ERIKA

Also by WILLIAM HEYEN

Depth of Field   (1970)
Noise in the Trees: Poems and a Memoir   (1974)
The Swastika Poems   (1977)
Long Island Light: Poems and a Memoir   (1979)
The City Parables   (1980)
Lord Drangonfly: Five Sequences   (1981)

A Profile of Theodore Roethke   (Editor, 1971)
American Poets in 1976   (Editor, 1976)

Erika

Poems of the Holocaust

William Heyen

THE VANGUARD PRESS, INC.   *New York*

Copyright © 1977 & 1984 by William Heyen
Published by Vanguard Press, Inc., 424 Madison Avenue, New York, N.Y. 10017.
Published simultaneously in Canada by Book Center, Inc., Beaulac Street,
Montreal, Quebec

Library of Congress Cataloging in Publication Data

Heyen, William, 1940-
    Erika, poems of the Holocaust.

    1. Holocaust, Jewish (1939-1945)—Poetry. I. Title.
PS3558.E85E7   1984   811'.54   83-14671
ISBN 0-8149-0875-6

Designer: Elizabeth Woll
Manufactured in the United States of America.

Acknowledgments

Grateful acknowledgment is made to the editors and publishers of the following periodicals and books in which most of these poems first appeared: *American Poetry Review* ("The Children") ; *The Carleton Miscellany* ("A Snapshot of My Father, 1928") ; *Harper's* ("This Night") ; *The Humanist* ("Simple Truths") ; *The Iowa Review* ("The Census," "A Visit to Belzec") ; *John Berryman Studies* ("Riddle") ; *Manassas Review* ("New Year's Eve: The Bridge") ; *Modern Poetry Studies* ("For Hermann Heyen") ; *The New Yorker* ("Stories") ; *The Ohio Review* ("Passover: The Injections," "The Swastika Poems") ; *The Ontario Review* (Parts I and III of "Three Relations," "Lament," "Men in History," "The Liberation Films," "Darkness," "The Uncertainty Principle") ; *Pembroke Magazine* ("On an Archaic Torso of Apollo") ; *Poetry East* (Part II of "Three Relations," "A New Bible") ; *Quarterly Review of Literature* ("For Wilhelm Heyen") ; *Rapport* ("I Dream of Justice") ; *Skywriting* ("Nocturne: The Reichsführer at Stutthof") ; *The Southern Review* ("The Numinous"). Some poems have been revised since first publication.

"The Children" also appeared as a chapbook in England from Sceptre Press in 1979. "Darkness" was first published as a chapbook by Rook Press in 1977. "For Wilhelm Heyen" and "For Hermann Heyen" also appeared, in different versions, in *Depth of Field* (Baton Rouge: Louisiana State University Press, 1970). A shorter version of "Erika" appeared in *Strivers' Row*. "The Trench" was originally published as a broadside by Rook Press. "Kotov," "The Hair: Jacob Korman's Story," "Dark in the Reich of the Blond," and "My Holocaust Songs" first appeared in *My Holocaust Songs* (Concord, N.H.: William B. Ewert, 1980). "The Trains," "The Legacy," and "Poem Touching the Gestapo" first appeared in *The Trains* (Worcester, Ma.: Metacom Press, 1981).

The author would also like to thank the State University of New York College at Brockport for a sabbatical during which this book came together in its final form.

Contents

When, after about ten years, I finished *The Swastika Poems* (1977), I thought I was done writing about that world of the Holocaust and the Third Reich. But even while my book was in proof, other such poems began to surface. These, I believe, add necessary voices and angles, deepen themes and positions, and I've attempted to integrate them with those that appeared in the earlier book. I hope now to have reached the questioning silence of the final poem here.

W. H.

The supreme tragic event of modern times is the murder of the six million European Jews. In a time which has not lacked in tragedies, this event most merits that unenviable honor—by reason of its magnitude, unity of theme, historical meaningfulness, and sheer opaqueness. . . Ultimately, the only response is to continue to hold the event in mind, to remember it. This capacity to assume the burden of memory is not always practical. Sometimes remembering alleviates grief or guilt; sometimes it makes it worse. Often, it may not do any good to remember. But we may feel that it is right, or fitting, or proper. This moral function of remembering is something that cuts across the different worlds of knowledge, action and art.

—SUSAN SONTAG

I dreamed I had a lovely fatherland.
The sturdy oak
Grew tall there, and the violets gently swayed.
Then I awoke.

I dreamed a German kiss was on my brow,
And someone spoke
The German words: "I love you!" (How they rang!)
Then I awoke.

HEINRICH HEINE
TR. AARON KRAMER

1/MEN IN HISTORY

Stories

I

A few hours before Heinrich,
my father's father, drowned in the North Sea
in nineteen-twenty at twenty-eight, he
walked outside his small home at Aurich

to pack his nets, spread on hedges to dry
in the German sun. My father, ten,
helped double, and double them again,
hand to hand, eye to blue eye

with his father who would soon be dead.
The horse-drawn wagon drew away. The fisherman
waved farewell to his wife and three sons.
My father, as he always did, tossed

an apple to the rider who, this morning,
backlit, rode silhouette against the sun.
Heinrich's shade dropped the apple, the fortune
in eel, fluke, and mackerel it meant to bring.

This simple world of signs went on. The wind-ripped
brine-tinged fields lay fallow, small flounders
dozed at low tide under the stars
in the mud flats until, at daylight, speared

by children. The hollow, the shadow, the dead whine,
the wrack father twisting at anchor in my father's chest,
the North Sea's black shine, the North Wind's lost
song, the painful windfalls—these diminished, but that son

who planed thin the blades of his father's ash oars
and mounted them where they have pointed fifty years
into the wind above that house—arrow, weathervane—
would be no fisherman. Now, on their way down

to the same ancestral sea,
the luckier Aurich sons know that Heinrich's soul
lives in the wind, his only home,
in the seawind. This is one story.

II

I remember walking with my father
near the blue spruce that smoldered in shade,
hunched and crushed at the edge of the wood,
but alive in the blocked Long Island light. He bent over

to tie the shoe I lifted to his knee.
I was so close, this once, that when
he looked up, I saw his left pupil widen,
fill with the blue-tipped green-black tree,

4

and swell with tears. When I dream of this,
I know, as I couldn't then, his two brothers
are just dead. I cup his tears
in my palm, as I didn't then, and the spruce

rises, from this water,
so blue, so light I am able to hold it
above us. The tree's perfect
form branches above us. This is another.

III

Wilhelm was killed in Holland,
Hermann over Russia. The North Sea's spawn
did not miss a rhythm when Berlin
burned to the ground.

What if the world is filled with stories?—
we hear only a few, live fewer,
and most that we live or hear
solve nothing, lead nowhere; but the spruce

appears again, rooted in dreamed tears,
yes, each branch, each needle
its own true story, yours,
mine, ours to tell.

A Snapshot of
My Father, 1928

His hick tie
flares out into the granular wind,
his thick kraut hair sprouts from under a cap you
wouldn't be caught dead in.

But he's smiling, he's
holding hard to the ship's rail,
and he won't let go because he's on his way now,
he's on his way to America,

a country he smelled
when the North Sea warmed to summer,
a country he saw when the story in a reader said
rivers, trees, land, money.

So he's eighteen, and somehow
he's on his way now. The Atlantic wind
blows his baggy trousers way out in front of him,
and he looks like famine,

this hayseed
with bad teeth, this carpenter

sporting a jacket patched at an elbow, this Dutchman
wearing a new life in his eyes.

But he doesn't know
what he looks like, or doesn't care,
but just cares to hold tight to the rail because
everything is all right,

he's on his way now,
my father, for richer or poorer,
smiling for fifty years now because he's going to make it
to America.

For Wilhelm Heyen

(d. 1940, buried in Holland)

I

The shaft of the film curls with smoke.
Within the camera's depth of field:

battalions of bone-white crosses
(the lines of a chaplain's gestures

in a pre-battle benediction)
and a still-living soldier

fronting them, and staring
into my eyes, into the dark. He waves.

The soldier moves his right arm.
This is, and was, certain in time.

II

The film shakes, and holds.
He chars at the edges, burns,

8

but the film moves. Holland
snows. White-tarpaulined trucks

lumber like polar bears.
Soldiers dig trenches,

stack shells, string
barbed wire with cans, plant

mines. Night falls. The wire
rattles. The mines flower.

III

Because these causes are never just,
rest, my twenty-year-old uncle, rest.

I'll say you walked with soldiers,
killed, were killed. The Dutch

cut the medals from your chest.
That book of love poems

my father said you pressed
out of your heart is also dust.

IV

Wilhelm, your face, a shadow
under your helmet,

fades from the gray air
of newsreels. You cannot hear

your nephew say your name.
I've seen you move your arm,

pendulum, scythe,
seen your hands cupped full with blood.

These are all your wars.
Asia trembles. You are never dead.

10

For Hermann Heyen

(*d. 1941 over Russia*)

Hermann, the Channel was blue-green
when you banked your plane and headed
back. But the Stuka's wing,
down which you sighted the countries you hated,
shone brilliant as medals,
didn't it? Your plane seemed
almost to be on fire, didn't it?

My Nazi uncle, you received the letters
my father still talks and wonders about—
the ones in which he told you to bail out
over England and plead insanity.
You got the letters, didn't you?
But you kept saying you'd land in London
with the rest of your squadron,

in a few months, when the war was over,
of course. Of course. But they needed you
in Russia, didn't they? And the few
who bailed out there were met by peasants
with pitchforks and scythes, weren't they?

Anyway, your plane blew up, for a moment,
like a sun; your dust bailed out all over.

Letter to
Hansjörg Greiner

(d. Oct. 20, 1944 at War Camp Arsk, the Urals)

I

Your wife once said
you marched to war
like a boy to school.

There is no rule.
She said no more.
She went to bed.

The American soldier she married,
half to get her children here,
half because he loved her,
still mutters and regrets
your years together.

Listen to a few more
footnotes to the war.
But what would you want to hear?

That your wife, martyred and noble,
welcomes your comrades to your German home?
Your family fled Berlin
down a corridor of flame.

That justice was done?
When the gas dropped in,
scapegoat Jews scratched their appeals
by bloody fingernails
on their shower stalls.

That your Fuehrer is alive and well
and still stands on balconies
waving to crowds?
He died by his own hand,
lives only for those whose histories
keep floating toward them like a cloud
risen from the Nazi furnace.

II

Has no one written you? Then I. You're
another one I don't know how
to talk to, but have to.

Stalingrader, it's now another spring
since the Russian winter of your capture.
Outside our shining windows

the year has turned again.
The daughter that you left
just old enough to know, and who,

now and again during our long winters
fingers the gold locket and bracelet
you gave her, now plants

a bed of flowers,
marigolds and zinnias that will soon
bloom in our yard.

But you will still be dead.

III

I suppose you'd stammer and shrug,
recall, if anything, the duel
that slashed your left cheek to the bone,

your marriage, and how it was
you met her, and how it was
to kiss her for the first time,

and how it was to walk the street,
a Wehrmacht officer with three children
whose hair the German sunlight

caressed like a hand.

14

IV

Lieutenant,
sometimes while walking,
or reading the papers, or driving
in traffic to work, we say your name

to ourselves in the slow syllables of prayer,
construct your face and posture from photographs
or the few moments we remember,
and from thin air.

For a few seconds, we close our eyes.
This is where you live,
in flashes of darkness
under our eyelids.

Men in History

I

Keitel *still* expected the secret weaponry
of deliverance, and maniacal Goering
even *now* angled for power.
Eva Braun, shadowy queen
of this black bower, resigned herself
to long hours of waiting
for cyanide, or one more night's love,

but over the Fuehrer's last days,
as Berlin crumbled above him
and a fine dust seemed
to cloud his bunkers, he moved
divisions of ghosts across maps,
and others around him
kept asking themselves
if this was all a dream.

Shriveled, insubstantial, unreal
even to himself, he walked

with an old peasant's stoop
in a uniform stained by food
dropped by his shaking hands.
Above him, his Reich's burnished eagle
lay in rubble, flew downward into flame.

II

But now it was mid-April,
his birthday, his fifty-sixth
year to heaven,
and since it was his last, and since
he knew, he left for the last time
his shelter and eventual tomb—
sixteen feet of concrete and six of earth—
for the Chancellery's upper rooms,

where walls peeled, drapes were down,
and paintings he'd insisted on
were long since packed away.
A hat lay in an easy chair,
old newspapers haunted the corridors.
This man shook hands, blustered,
passed out signed photographs of himself
framed in silver. Often nostalgia

floated him back twenty years until
his eyes brimmed with tears quickly
wiped away with the back of his hand.

III

Then it was over.
He took his leave, wound
back down to his bunker
to finish the war,
to wait for God to open
the iron gate of the sun
for one more soldier soon
to die. This architect, this

messiah, this man in history
would die just once,
would flame just once into a darkness
far past our spit and curses.
As he said to Albert Speer:
"Believe me, it is easy for me
to end my life. A brief moment
and I'm freed of everything."

IV

Born in Brooklyn of German parents,
I remember lines scratched on our doors,
the crooked swastikas my father cursed
and painted over. And I remember
the *Volksfest* at Franklin Square
on Long Island every summer—
stands of smoked eel, loaves

of dark bread, raffles, shooting galleries,
beer halls, bowling alleys,
boys in *lederhosen*
flooded by an ocean of guttural German
they never learned, or learned to disavow.
I remember hourly parades under the lindens,
the elders' white beards, the sad depths of their eyes.

I remember their talk of the North Sea,
the Rhine of Lorelei, Cologne's
twin towers, the Black Forest, the mountains,
the Hamelin piper who led everyone's children to nowhere.
But I, too, was a child: all those years
there was one word I never heard,
one name never mentioned.

Three Relations

I (Aachen, 1935)

He came to our city,
and the people were shouting and crying.
They hailed the Fuehrer
as the deliverer.
I was in the crowd, caught
in delirium, a moving box,
pushed forward.
Closer and closer he came
in the glistening black car
through a sea of heads.
The people almost touched him,
but I could not lift my arm.
And now he was opposite me,
and he gave me a look.
It was a look of death,
there was the chill of death in his white face.
I knew it, then:
he was the incarnation of death.
I felt it in my marrow.
All those who cried after him as their redeemer,

cried for death.
His look froze my heart,
and I raised my arm,
and I cried *heil*.

II (Released from Dachau, 1939)

. . . and then, after warnings

not to speak of what we'd seen,
we boarded the train. . . .

At last, it left the Munich station. . . .

In the compartment, we talked about our plans.
We couldn't sleep, although we were very tired. . . .

Vienna's houses emerged from fog. . . .

I went over to the toilet mirror,
adjusted my hat over my shorn hair. . . .

The train rolled in. I stepped down from the car.
There is my wife, pale and worn. . . .

At home, my little daughter clung to me and kissed me.
I felt afraid that I was in a dream,

I feel afraid that I am in a dream. . . .

III (Sachsenhausen, 1944)

The small stone house stands by itself,
thirty meters long, thirty meters wide,
five meters high. Two small windows
with heavy bars. A lawn in front,
and a wooden shack, where people undress,
to shower, they think.
They walk into the stone house.

Concrete floor and no furniture.
Maybe two hundred nozzles stick out.
The two windows and door lined with rubber.
It's a shower, all right, but gas comes out,
and twists their bodies into awful shapes.
Gas does not put them quietly to sleep.
Their flesh is torn with their own or others' teeth.

Their bodies were bluish red.
We dragged them out of the gas house
by hair and ears and feet
and threw them on a flat wagon.
Each wagon had room for seventy bodies.
We drove the load to the crematorium.
We stacked them at the entrance.

Flesh does not burn like wood—
it takes a long time to burn humans.
Burning seventy or eighty corpses every day—
it's slow going.
There is always a fire in the ovens.
Day and night
a whitish smoke blows out of the chimney.

A New Bible

He told me his story, and today I have forgotten it, but it was certainly a sorrowful, cruel and moving story; because so are all our stories, hundreds of thousands of stories, all different and all full of a tragic, disturbing necessity. We tell them to each other in the evening, and they take place in Norway, Italy, Algeria, the Ukraine, and are simple and incomprehensible like the stories in the Bible. But are they not themselves stories of a new Bible?

—Primo Levi

The lamp was a gift from a friend at Auschwitz. It now stands on an end-table in an *SS* officer's apartment at Bergen-Belsen.

It is evening. The lamp is lit. It glows softly, gives off barely enough light to read by. You and I are there as children, reading a book by the light of that lamp.

Our parents are getting ready for a party. They pass back and forth in front of us. The lamp shadows them against the walls.

We are reading a story from a new Bible. We are as quiet as the shadows.

In the story we are now reading, a master orders the children to come to him. They leave their trains at a station where a clock is painted on false walls. It is always three o'clock. The master is a shadow. In two hours, at three o'clock, the children are ashes.

There is no end to this book. It begins again, with other stories, after its last page. The lamp seems to concentrate its light on our book.

In the yellow glow of the lamp on the pages of our story, we see other colors, mauves, rose. When we look up at the lampshade, we see Erika blossoms, and a rose, through which the bulb shines.

We turn the page. It is three o'clock. So many trains converge on the station, so many stories.

Passover:
The Injections

Clouds pass over, endless,
black fruit dripping
sap from the branches
of lightning.

We lie down in the field,
thousands of us,
never mind the rain.

Soldiers come toward us,
groups of three or four.
The wind opens their long coats.
Underneath, their uniforms are black.

They bend over to the babies.
The babies cry,
for a little while.

"We are living in Biblical times,"
a woman says.

Nocturne: The Reichsführer at Stutthof

All night the current
buzzes and crackles
through the barbed wire
around his camp.
Commandant Himmler,
in his sandstone house—
white, clean, rectangular—
dreams back to the murmur
of childhood pines,
to the murmur of the sea.
When he awakens and hears the wire,
he says to himself, Heinrich,
sometimes, in this life
you have found and made,
you are so happy
your heart wants to burst.

The Car

He said he'd save
just enough Jews
to fill one car.

He said he'd drive
that car himself
through the cities.

Last stop: Berlin.
Citizens throng
to see the Jews

his mercy spared.
Berliners count:
one, two . . . three, four.

Each Jew thinks he
or she will be
among the four.

The Hair: Jacob Korman's Story

Ten kilometers from Warsaw,
I arrived in Rembertow where
hundreds of Jews had lived
until the wheel turned: *Judenrein*.

You think they let themselves be taken?
They would not fill the trucks.
Men were shot trying to pull guns
from the guards' hands,

and hands of dead women
clutched hair, hair of *SS* guards,
blood-patched hair everywhere,
a *velt mit hor*, a field of hair.

The Funnel: Speech to Jews at Treblinka by Kurt Franz

Why try to run? Why take risks? No matter
how far you flee, you return
to Treblinka,

a funnel whose upper edges are the ends of earth. You
are near the bottom. Others are already
falling, falling
fast,

will pass you soon. Do not run from your
responsibilities. The earth
will be purged
of Jews,

and Treblinka will become for you a world of joy.
I swear this on my honor
as an *SS*.

Dark in the Reich
of the Blond

I had my papers, but I was running.
I had my proof, but I was running.
I had my trees of Aryan descent,
but I was running,

but I'd been dreaming,
and woke beneath a pile of corpses.
I was happy, hidden,
and I had my papers.

The moon shone down, but I was hiding.
The stars winked down, but I was hiding.
The sky had eyes, and they were open,
but I was hiding.

I am here now, where you are, too.
I live here now, where you will, too.
We two will wait here, quiet, still,
while the night forgets. . . .

Do you have your papers? Lie here quiet.
Let the eyes run down like rain, let
the bodies turn to grass
as we wait here with our papers. Lie here quiet.

Kotov

Ivan Ivanovitch Kotov, short of speech,
clarity drifting away to mindlessness—
Kotov of stutter and suddenly empty eyes—
only Kotov, in all Russia, of all those locked inside,
survived the *dushegubka,*
the murder wagon, the gas van. Only Kotov,

pushed with his new bride
into the seatless seven-ton gray truck,
stood on that grated floor, and lived. Only Kotov,
pressed together with fifty others, would wake
in the ditch of dead, half buried, and crawl away.
He'd smelled gas, torn off one sleeve,
soaked it in his urine, covered nose and mouth,

lost consciousness, and lived, waking
in a pit of bodies somewhere outside of Krasnodar.
His wife?—he could not find her.
Except for the dead, he was alone. . . .
He stood up, staggered and groped through fields
back to the city, where he hid until the end.

Only Kotov, saved by his own brain and urine, woke
from that wedding in the death van,
in Russia, in the time of that German invention,
the windowless seven-ton gray *dushegubka.*

A History of Germany
under National Socialism

Even Carin Goering's ideal
Aryan skull in the rubble.

Other Men in History

Berlin, the *Kaiserhof,* a few years ago:
"If only Paulus had broken out!"
The speaker's brown beer flashed red
as the blood that melted snow at Stalingrad.

"We'd still have had them by their throats!"
Others at his table nodded.
"Now they are all dead, dead,
three hundred thousand of our finest *SS* studs."

Riddle

From Belsen a crate of gold teeth,
from Dachau a mountain of shoes,
from Auschwitz a skin lampshade.
Who killed the Jews?

Not I, cries the typist,
not I, cries the engineer,
not I, cries Adolf Eichmann,
not I, cries Albert Speer.

My friend Fritz Nova lost his father—
a petty official had to choose.
My friend Lou Abrahms lost his brother.
Who killed the Jews?

David Nova swallowed gas,
Hyman Abrahms was beaten and starved.
Some men signed their papers,
and some stood guard,

and some herded them in,
and some dropped the pellets,

and some spread the ashes,
and some hosed the walls,

and some planted the wheat,
and some poured the steel,
and some cleared the rails,
and some raised the cattle.

Some smelled the smoke,
some just heard the news.
Were they Germans? Were they Nazis?
Were they human? Who killed the Jews?

The stars will remember the gold,
the sun will remember the shoes,
the moon will remember the skin.
But who killed the Jews?

The Trains

Signed by Franz Paul Stangl, Commandant,
there is in Berlin a document,
an order of transmittal from Treblinka:

248 freight cars of clothing,
400,000 gold watches,
25 freight cars of women's hair.

Some clothing was kept, some pulped for paper.
The finest watches were never melted down.
All the women's hair was used for mattresses, or dolls.

Would these words like to use some of that same paper?
One of those watches may pulse in your own wrist.
Does someone you know collect dolls, or sleep on human hair?

He is dead at last, Commandant Stangl of Treblinka,
but the camp's three syllables still sound like freight cars
straining around a curve, Treblinka,

Treblinka. Clothing, time in gold watches,
women's hair for mattresses and dolls' heads.
Treblinka. The trains from Treblinka.

To the Onlookers

(*after Nelly Sachs*)

When our backs are turned,
when someone stares at us,
we feel them.
You who watched the killing, and did nothing,
still feel the eyes of those dead
on your bodies.

How many see you
as you pick a violet?
How many oak branches twist
into hands begging for help?
How many memories congeal
in the sun's evening blood?

O the unsung cradlesongs
in the dove's nightcries—
so many would have loved
their own stars in the night skies,
but now only the old well
can do it for them.

You did not murder,
but looked on, you,
who could have been changed
into light.

The Census

Something happened: this is history,
of course. But how to feel it,
and who cares? Example:
November 17th, 1934, at Terezin,

day of the infamous census,
the *SS* inventing a need to know
how many Jews they had, herding
maybe 40,000 into a muddy field

to wait all day without food or water.
Planes circled overhead. Machine guns
guarded the edges, an evening
of shrieking children. At midnight,

Jews ordered back to barracks,
never mind 300 dead
as the cold mud. . . .
We've heard this before,

even have a painting, *The Census*,
by Leo Haas, filled with darkness
and the silence whereby/
wherein we witness, yes,

40

but I've read this twice, this
history, and here in my own words
the same Holocaust problem, and luck:
no one, never mind me,

can quite catch it,
not even those surviving that field
can feel it, not even now
as they trace numbers on their wrists,

not even though we cry,
as we do. And we don't truly
want to, unless we want to die.
I, for one, speak this

from a safe place, the green woods
darkening around me with history,
yes, but safely. November
as I speak, yes, bringing

these memories on again,
but I'm warm here, and can leave.
Even Terezin recedes, relentless,
gray milk of the afternoon,

of grandma's hair.
This is the census:
the lost are too many,
and are lost. So

we strain to, or say so,
but cannot quite remember.
What about the mid-January 1945
forced march of 64,000 prisoners

across Poland from Auschwitz
to the camp whose name
curses a beech wood?
50,000 died. We

want to live. Who
ever wanted to know the truth
about transports to the East
from Terezin? Those who knew they

might be chosen the next day,
tried to sleep, or hum music,
or pray. . . . Still, it was November,
a trace of snow in that field where Israel

waited to be counted
in the milky light. Overcast,
and planes circling like ravens,
but you and I are still alive,

or are we? We know what happened
at Terezin, seventeen November
1943. This is close enough. We
can't kill the guards,

though we might wish to. Most
moved away, died natural deaths,
or have retired into history. We
can't take the prisoners' places,

or promise the dead that that field
won't be used that way again.
But Leo Haas is there,
and the next day will paint

the field of Jews. Now,
I've his painting in a book,
can turn to it as often as I want to,
which won't be often—

will *you* go out of *your* way
to look for it?
We make do.
We do what we can, or want to,

and each day numbers us
further away, unless history
circles closer,
as it may.

We change our pronouns,
and tenses. We change our names,
or say them until they
wear away. We live. We walk

from the field at Terezin.
Even those who make history
shovelling corpses into ovens
sleep, and will not/cannot

feel their actions.
Do I follow me?
Who wants to hunker down
in that field again? Why live there

when we can live more easily
in history? . . .
Still, no matter where I've
talked to, I want to show you, to say

"here, here it was, here."
And you'd *like*,
as long as you were passing time here,
to be led there, where they were,

in threadbare coats, or coatless,
some shoeless. . . . Here we are,
then: cold enough
for the prisoners' breath

to mist the air. Droning
shadows overhead.
1943. November the 17th.
Terezin. This is our history

despite the Nazis.
East means Auschwitz.
Part of the census.
As true as we can be.

A Voice from the Night at Belsen

Give me back my jewels.
The mad girl climbed from one pallet to another,
crying for her jewels. Now, here,

in another world, a pearl moon
rounds the night air as we remember. The dead girl
becomes one of the jewels she cried for.

46

I Dream of Justice

In old Prussian law, three categories of thieves are specified: of gold, of horses, and of bees. . . . It may have been this clarification of natural law which stirred the mind of the nomad, rousing in him an inchoate perception of order and continuity.

—Kay Boyle

I

You who are poor, take back your coins.
You who are Jews, take back your teeth.
You who are shorn, take back your hair.
You who were brave, you who collapsed in terror,
you who are dead, take back all the lost days of sunlight,
for I have hanged the thief of gold.

II

Farmers, back to your herds,
for the steel tanks they sired are lost,
and the sharks that glide under the waters:
cavalry vanished into the red wind,
the tanks flamed back to black ore,
the submarines burst like lungs.
Take back your herds,
for I have hanged the thief of horses.

III

The thief of bees thought,
when your bees swarmed,
they had gathered for battle.
Take back your hives,
which bore him such bitter honey,
for I have hanged the thief of bees.

IV

I have awakened.
What is it I have come to?
Far outside this morning's window
horses graze their meadow,
and the bright air around the trees is strung
with golden necklaces of bees.

Darkness

Thirty, fifty, eighty years later,
it's getting darker.
The books read, the testimonies all taken,
the films seen through the eye's black lens,
darker. The words
remember: Treblinka green,
Nordhausen red,
Auschwitz blue, Mauthausen
orange, Belsen white—
colors considered
before those places named themselves. Thirty,
fifty, eighty years later. Now
the camps—I lose them—
where are they? Darker.
If it is true
that I've always loved him,
darker. If it is true
that I would kill again,
darker. If it is true
that nothing matters,
darker. If it is true
that I am jealous of them,

the Nazis' hooked crosses, the Jews' stripes . . .
He speaks inside me. Darker.
I lie on a table
in the Fuehrer's bunker,
outside his chamber,
in the hall. I am waiting.
They do not see me,
dogs nor people. This
dream begins again, the film
circles and burns. Eighty, fifty,
thirty years. Darker. He
touched my forehead. He
speaks now, says, somehow,
lower, tells me to speak to the lower power,
for once, to say,
come back, enter, I was once alive.
Darker. The air
swims with words, hair
twines the words, numbers
along a wrist, along
a red brick shower. Darker.
To forgive them,
killer and victim: darker.
Doctor, help me kill
the Goebbels children. Darker.
Across the street, now,
a cattlecar, stalled.
The skin lampshades darken under varnish.
Fragments. Can I call
him back? Millions still
call him back in deepest prayer,

but the light diffused
as spray, past
Andromeda, in spiral
shadows. Darker, always
darker. *SS*, death's head,
oval hollow deadface hole for boot—
fragments. The heroes
all dead in the first five minutes.
Darker. To enter
this darkness, to dig
this chancellery garden to my own
remains, to watch
as the black face and scrotum
lacking one egg stare up
at the sun, to speak
with that charred jaw,
carrying this with me. Darker.
Underneath the answer, under
the darkness, this love I have,
this lust to press these words.
He tells me *lower,*
and the black breastbone aches with it,
the last black liquid
cupped in the eyesockets smells of it,
odor of cyanide's bitter almond,
the viscera smeared to the backbone
shines with it, for me
to say it all, my
hands around his neck,
mouth to mouth, my lips
to kiss his eyes to sleep. We

will taste this history together,
my friend: take a deep breath.
Take it. Smell
almond in the air.
The leader lives.

The Legacy

I am alive. Those Jews are dead.
I am living. They are dead.
I think of them. They are dead.
I think of them. They are dead.
I think of one. He wants to speak.
I think of him. He makes a sound.
I hear his sound. He moans.
I hear him moan. He is dying.
I am alive. He is dying.
I am living. They are dying.
I think of them. They are dead.
I think of one. She is dead.
I think of her. She makes a sound.
I hear her sound. She makes an *r* sound.
I hear her sound. She repeats the *r*.
I remember them. They are dead.
I remember his moan. He is dead.
I remember her *r*. She is dead.
I remember them. They make sounds.
I remember them. They die.
I remember them. They are making sounds.
I dream of them. They sing.
I hear them sing. They sing together.

I hear their song.   Their song is mine.
I smell of almond.   They smell of almond.
I die with them.   They live with me.
I leave to meet them.   They come to meet me.
I am dying.   They are living.
I am dying.   They are singing.
I am dead.   They are living.
I am dead.   They are singing.
I am dead.   They are living.
I am alive.   They are dead.
I am dead.   They are dead.
I am dead.   They are dead.
I am dead.   They are dead.

2/ERIKA

Erika

They were points of transit, they offered impressions whose essence could not be held steady, was always vanishing, and when I inquire what there is about them that cannot be stressed and found valuable, to give a firm position in the topography of my life, I keep on coming up against what keeps retreating from me, all those cities become blurs, and only one place, where I spent only one day, remains constant.

—Peter Weiss

Buchenwald: a beech wood, a soft word shining with sunlight falling through yellow leaves. A name, a place of terror. *Ravensbrück:* bridge of the ravens, a word out of the medieval gloom. *Dachau, Auschwitz:* words with no, so far as I know, particular root meanings, but words that leave us confounded and inconsolable. And *Bergen-Belsen.* The name whines like a missile or jet engine. It is a name from which there is no escape. And it is impossible to imagine what happened at Belsen.

It happens that my earliest memories are of 1945. I was five. We lived in Woodhaven, on Long Island. My father worked in the shipyards, building against the Axis. I remember the green gate in front of our house and what the houses on our street looked like and how close together they were. I remember a trellis that leaned against one side of our garage. I remember, though I did not know what it was at that time, the persecution we suffered because we were Germans, the swastikas my father scraped from our windows or painted over when they appeared suddenly in the mornings on our steps or doors. 1945. At Belsen, as the trees began to leaf that spring, Jews and other dissidents were being murdered by the thousands. I remember the day in 1945 that Franklin

57

Roosevelt died. I remember that day because my brother and I were getting ready to go to the movies when my mother came outside and said we couldn't go because the President had died and the movies were closed. I remember that day because I was bitterly disappointed. And that day, because Roosevelt had died, down in his Berlin bunker Hitler was pounding his fist on a table and assuring himself that God had sent him a sign, that Roosevelt's death meant the Third Reich would now rise from the rubble. And that same day, children no older than I were being put to death at Belsen.

Belsen is forty miles north of Hannover, out of the way, and was meant to be. You are not likely to visit the place, but if you do, if you find the signs to *Gedenkstatte Bergen-Belsen* and find the place and park in the lot outside the grounds, you will walk under pines past a caretaker's apartment to which the central building, a square and simple affair of glass and stone, is attached. From the outside it looks like a small art gallery, perhaps, or a gymnasium. You will pause outside its glass doors to read a sign whose legend outlines the camp's history.

In 1940 Belsen, an already existing barracks, became a prisoner-of-war camp, Stalag 311. Russian captives were quartered there when a massive epidemic of spotted fever swept the camp. April of 1943 saw the establishment of the so-called Detention Camp Bergen-Belsen; Jews began to be collected there. In March of 1944 people who were no longer able to work were transferred to Belsen from other camps. In October and November of 1944 eight thousand women arrived from Auschwitz-Birkenau. A month later, the latter camp's *SS* Commandant, Joseph Kramer, took charge at Belsen. The camp grew rapidly, apace with his ambition. Within a year after Kramer's arrival the camp grew from fifteen thousand to sixty thousand prisoners, many of whom came from camps too near the front.

Belsen's last year was absolute hell. Nine thousand were executed there during the first two weeks of April, 1945. In the middle of that April the British arrived to liberate the camp, but despite their best efforts conditions were such that an additional nine thousand died during the next two weeks. Eighteen thousand died during that terrible April. While I was playing in the Woodhaven streets, six hundred people a day died at Belsen. The sign outside the memorial building concludes with the estimate that at least fifty thousand had been murdered at the camp. Anne Frank, who wrote that she needed only sunlight to hope, was one of them.

You are not likely to visit the place, but if you do, and if you are there in December, as I was, you will walk inside into a single big room. The room will be dark and cold. You will find no bones, hair, teeth, lampshades made of tattooed skin there, and for this you will be thankful. But you will see a map that locates what were German concentration camps and their surrounding cells and satellites. The map is a spiderweb of camps, stations, deployment centers. Then you will see the photographs that cover the stone walls, images you've seen so often before: the mummified bodies, the Lugers held against the temples of old men, the huge eyes, the common graves from which arms and legs sprout like mushrooms. But this time these photographs are of the very place where you are standing; this is a dimension you have not entered before.

In one photograph smoke rises from the center of the camp above barbed wire and shacks and pines. In another, you will see only the backs of seven women who stand above their graves for a last few seconds of life as the photographer trips his shutter. These are young women who must not have been at the camp for long: their hair seems luxurious, and they are not thin. Their dresses seem to billow slightly behind them, their hair seems slightly blown back from a wind blowing toward the camera. Now, as the seven women stand there above that ditch, their hands bound behind their backs, they can see dozens of bodies below them, perhaps the bodies of their husbands and children. For a few seconds, as the photographer arranged his equipment or simply brought his camera into focus, the women may have glanced up at the sky. They may have spoken to one another. They must have prayed. A few seconds after they stood up in the light and air and wind for a last time, they fell forward into the darkness. They are still falling.

On another wall in this room you will see blow-ups of newspaper descriptions of the conditions the British troops found here in the spring of 1945. They had to burn the place to the ground as quickly as possible because they feared an epidemic. Corpses were hanging out of windows. The dead had to be buried in a hurry. There was no time for more than cursory identification procedures. The machine of the camp had run down as the British had advanced. Records were no doubt being destroyed, no doubt the German officers and guards were making their own plans, no doubt the murder of the last nine thousand they had time to murder those first two weeks in April was an inconvenience. This was Nazi *Kultur*.

You will walk outside past the mass graves. Each grave has a concrete marker: *Hier Ruhen 800 Tote April 1945; Hier Ruhen 1,000 Tote April 1945; Hier Ruhen 2,000 Tote April 1945*. The graves are banked at their bases by a band of about two feet of stone, and then the earth curves and slopes upward, rising as high as your head. The mounds are shaped something like loaves of bread, but squarer, flatter.

You might say to yourself: *They are really here. I am at Belsen, and these are the graves of people who were murdered here. This is the camp at Belsen.*

You will see that the graves are covered, as is the whole area, with Erika. Erika, bell-heather, *heide,* a heath plant, wild and strong. Wild and strong, and beautiful. When not in bloom Erika is green, a deep green. There is a poem by the German poet Hermann Löns, who died at Verdun, that begins: "Grün ist die Heide, / Die Heide ist grün." In December, Belsen is green, a dark green. But in early fall, I am told, Erika blooms a reddish blue or bluish red, and then Belsen must be very beautiful, the sun perhaps occasionally breaking through the cloud cover, a warmer wind perhaps rustling the stiff blooming Erika over the graves, the *heide*'s billions of flowerlets veiling the open spaces in shifting mauves and orchids and blue-purple shadows. It must be very beautiful and very terrible at Belsen when each fall the Erika blossoms. I do not think I will ever live a fall day when I do not think of Belsen. I will be driving to work, or opening a window, or playing cards with friends, or reading, and I will think of Erika blowing green or blooming violet-red over the dead at Belsen. And whenever I see a starling, or crow, I will remember the crows that stroke their black wings against the wind at Belsen.

Bergen-Belsen is not a big place, and it isn't old: what happened there happened shortly before mid-century. And it isn't a complicated place. It is very simple. At the edge of the camp there is a shaft of white marble. The words incised on it are simple and direct, and eloquent. Its fifth and sixth words are painted blood-red: Israel and the World *Shall Remember* Thirty Thousand Jews Exterminated in the Concentration Camp of Bergen-Belsen by the Hands of the Murderous Nazis." And further down on the stone: "Earth Conceal Not the Blood Shed on Thee!" Bergen-Belsen is a simple place, but it is more eloquent than the cathedral at Köln. It is a simple place, and it is easy to remember: there may be just a few days a year when the Erika is covered with snow, but in the early fall it blooms in the shades of lilac, the blossom of memory.

And I will always remember speaking to the caretaker at Belsen. He said that he still finds things there. When spring breaks he tills the soil or replaces a brick along a walk or transplants a tree or rakes through the Erika and finds

> a rusty spoon,
>   or a tin cup,
> or a fragment of bone,
>
> or a strand of barbed wire,
>   or a piece of rotten board,
> or the casing of a bullet,
>
> or the heel of a shoe,
>   or a coin,
> or a button,
>
> or a bit of leather
>   that crumbles to the touch,
> or a pin,
>
> or the twisted frames of someone's glasses,
>   or a key,
> or a wedding band.

3/THE NUMINOUS

The Baron's Tour

Gaze down at the Rhine.
I remember it red
with Roman blood.
We have always lived in this castle.

This is the room of trophies:
deer, griffin, boar, bear,
the long hair
and leathery scalp of a chinawoman.
Dragon, wolf, lampshade of jewskin.
We have always lived in this castle.

At the base of this stair, a door
opens to the Fuehrer's chamber.
In its center stand
candelabras of eternal flames.

We have thought to leave here,
but the labyrinthine passages,
the sheer plunge to the river,
the stones that have come to caress us . . .

This is the hall once lined
by hearts impaled on pikes.
These are the stair rails
of russian bone.
This is the turret
where the books are burned.

Come, see where kings entered
the grained wood of the oak bed
where you will sleep tonight.
One said he'd dreamed

of his whole courtyard filled with heads
whose eyes mirrored
fields inside of fields inside
of fields forever.
We have always
lived in this castle.

The Fountain

In a shady corner of the park [at Treblinka] an ornamental lake was dug and in the center was placed a stone frog, sculpted by prisoners, from whose open mouth a fountain was made to spout.
                                        —*Jean-Francois Steiner*

We will all
now see
the reflecting pool,
the fountain:
blood,
skin,
pus,
bones, crushed
hearts,
brains,
hair,
excrement,
and Jewish stars,
forever

The Spire

Wherever I am, I am not supposed to be here. I am above the street, above cobblestones shining the black shine of night and rain. It is cold, but in this dream I cannot feel the cold, and wherever I am, I know, I have been here a long time. Great dark shapes hang in the air behind me. Bells. A spire, a fretwork of porous red stone rises above me. Bodiless, I am in the belltower of the cathedral above the square at Freiburg. I have been here for centuries. I am breathing the air that flows around the still clappers of the great bells. The square below is empty. I have lived in this air, I know, since before the spire.

Something is about to happen. A straining of ropes, chains. The bells' clappers begin to slam against cold iron. Pigeons lift their black bodies into the air. It is as though the bells are inside me, as though they are echoing deeply and mournfully the sounds for dead, dead.

It is winter here, a drizzle of sleet sifting through the dark red fretwork of the spire, through the sound of the bells. In the east, toward the forest, the horizon whitens with dawn. Lord, help me, I cry, and awaken.

Blue

They were burning something. A lorry drew up at the pit and de-
livered its load—little children. Babies! Yes, I saw it—saw it with my
own eyes . . . those children in the flames. . . . I pinched my face.
Was I still alive? Was I awake? I could not believe it. . . . Never
shall I forget the little faces of the children, whose bodies I saw
turned into wreaths of smoke beneath a silent blue sky.

—*Elie Wiesel*

To witness, to
enter this
essence, this
silence, this
blue, color
of sky, wreaths
of smoke, bodies
of children blue
in their nets
of veins: a lorry
draws up at the pit
under the blue sky where
wreaths rise. These
are the children's bodies, this
our earth. Blue. A lorry
draws up at the pit
where children smolder. The sky
deepens into blue, its
meditation, a blue
flame, the children
smolder. Lord of blue,
blue chest and blue brain,

a lorry of murdered children
draws up at the pit. This
happened, this
happens, Your
sign, children
flaming in their rags, children
of bone-smolder, scroll
of wreaths on Your blue
bottomless sky, children
rising wreathed
to Your blue lips.

The Liberation Films

Seeing the films:
now we begin to know.

A bulldozer working the piles of dead together,
its treads hacking horizontal ladders

into this remorseless German dirt
that translates flesh into Erika and flowers:

now we begin to know.
Now we begin to know.

Seeing the dozer's curved blade curl
the dead like a flesh wave

as high as our heads
toward great necessary pits;

seeing the bodies white
with necessary lime;

seeing the bodies fall
over the graves' edges;

seeing the eyes staring at nothing,
the bodies falling in slow motion;

seeing the stick limbs falling in slow motion:
now we begin to know.

Seeing the dead roll and fall
as though flailing their last air,

without words, without sound,
without one syllable of their last prayers:

now we begin to know You, Lord,
now we begin to know.

The Angel Hour

As I chew my morning cereal,
I remember the camps,
how victims tried to live on infected water,
their own diminishing bodies,
their will to bear witness.
In my fantasy, God is retroactive,
gives them one hour each day free from fear.
They will call it "the angel hour."
They will each have a bowl of cereal,
wheat flakes with nuts and raisins and dates
drenched in milk. They will eat slowly
when even the SS must cower and whisper,
die Engelstunde. . . .
In this way, I save so many,
as I chew my morning cereal.

The Trench

This is Verdun,
horizon of barbed wires
lit with flares.
Shudder of mortar on both flanks, and now
down the dreamed line the repeated scream:
gas. My thick fingers,
my mask unstraps slowly and heavily from my pack,
a fumble of straps,
buckles, tubes.
I try to hold my breath,
and now the mask is on,
smells of leather and honeysuckle vomit.
The poison smoke
drifts into the trench,
settles. My neck
strains to hold up the mask.
I will.
Behind this pane of isinglass
I am ready,
my bayonet fixed for the first black shape
to fill trenchlight above me and fall.
I know that all my life one

German soldier has plunged toward me
over the bodies of the lost.
I am ready for him.
We are both wearing masks,
and only one of us will live.

Lines to My Parents

(*Hannover, 1971–72*)

I

A few days ago,
I saw those Bremerhaven graves.
Unadorned stones
honor our simpler dust.

I almost knelt to save
a leaf of ivy. I even heard
the dead were glad
that I'd returned.

But will you understand?
I was content to watch
the North Sea's wind
wearing away our names.

II

Will you understand?
Canes and armless coats
haunt these German streets
I force myself to walk.

Factories smoke the sky,
and in the absurd cause-
effect of night,
I lie half-asleep

dreaming of thirty years ago.
Below my windows
old soldiers tap the cobblestones,
stop, stare into the mist-

white air; widows
who have worn their weeds
for thirty years, hurry
to nowhere in the steady rain.

III

Last night, at last, I met him,
inside a glade of oaks,
and touched his iron helmet,
and scratched his mossy face.

I stepped inside a clearing,
I walked the hallowed ground.
I found an iron soldier where
a drumbeat seemed to roll.

Nor consecration, nor cathedral,
nor clouds that Jehovah wove,
but rain beat down like shrapnel
through the dead leaves.

Say he drives the wind, father,
say he stares from the sun.
Say he cries like the crows
beating the sky at Belsen.

Say his tears are the rain, mother,
say I have been his brother.
Say his medals are the moon,
say you have been his lover.

IV

My thirty-
first birthday broke with sun
and dried the counter-
clockwise whirl of water

down the drains:
I walked the woods again,
but now alone
in the pine, oak,

and linden autumn.
Once more the leaves
had turned to flame;
gray doves

weighed down the highest limbs;
rabbits burst
across my paths
as they do at home.

V

Say he is molded from nothing, mother,
say he is nowhere.
Say he has not returned,
say he will never.

Say that your brothers died, father,
say that they never lived.
Say you cannot read the writing
below his metal head.

Say he is in the bells
echoing down the air.
Say he haunts the Erika
forty miles from here.

Say when I hear the bells
from forty miles away,
they say the Jews have risen
from where the forests burn.

They say the Jews have risen
from where the forests burn.

Two Walks

I

(Through the Night with My Father, 1945)

One of them is yours, my father said.
I looked, but into too much heaven
for me to find which part was mine.
It's exactly overhead,

and always will be. See it, there,
the one that seems to see you?
He was right. I saw it burning near
(planet born when I was born), and blue.

II

(At Bergen-Belsen, 1971)

Morning, while Erika blew green from mound
to mound, the man who works at Belsen
raked a rusted wire from the ground.
Noon, I walk among the thousands dead, hear

crows cry *rawr, rawr* through the dark air.
I watch them drift to nowhere down the wind,
but see we still throw shadows here, my fathers,
my crows, my black immortal stars.

Lament

(after Rilke)

O how everything deceives,
like my star
of black light, dead
in the heavens
for thousands of years!
I break into tears
at the cold words
from the boat of stars
that passes over, and over.
Where in my body
does the same clock beat?
I would like to walk
away from my heart.
I would like to pray
under the dead sky,
if there were one star
which does not lie,
which endures,
a white city
at the end of its beam,
forever.

Mandorla

(after Celan)

In the almond—what dwells in the almond?
Absence.
It's absence dwells in the almond.
It dwells and it dwells.

In absence—who dwells there? The King.
There dwells the King, the King.
He dwells and He dwells.

    Jewish locks, you do not gray.

And your eye—where does your eye dwell?
Your eye dwells on the almond.
Your eye, it dwells on absence.
It dwells on the King.
This dwells and this dwells.

    Human locks, you do not gray.
    Empty almond, King's blue.

Death Fugue

(after Celan)

Black milk of daybreak we drink it evenings
we drink it middays and mornings we drink it nights
we drink and we drink
we shovel a grave in the air where there's room for us all
A man lives in the house he plays with serpents he writes
he writes when it darkens to Germany your golden hair
    Margarete
he writes and he steps from the house and it blazes the stars
       he whistles his pack to come forth
he whistles his Jews forth lets them shovel a grave in the earth
he commands us play for the dance

Black milk of daybreak we drink you nights
we drink you mornings and middays we drink you evenings
we drink and we drink
A man lives in the house and plays with serpents he writes
he writes when it darkens to Germany your golden hair
    Margarete
your ashen hair Shulamith we shovel a grave in the air
       where there's room for us all

He shouts slash deeper in earth you there you others sing and
    play
he grabs for the iron in his belt he swings his eyes are blue
slash deeper you with the spades you others play on for the
    dance

Black milk of daybreak we drink you nights
we drink you middays and mornings we drink you evenings
we drink and we drink
a man lives in the house your golden hair Margarete
your ashen hair Shulamith he plays with serpents

He shouts play sweeter to death death is a master from
    Germany
he shouts play darker the strings then rise as smoke into air
then you've a grave in the clouds where there's room for us all

Black milk of morning we drink you nights
we drink you middays death is a master from Germany
we drink you evenings and mornings we drink and we drink
death is an expert from Germany his eye is blue
he shoots you with bullets of lead he shoots you precisely
a man lives in the house your golden hair Margarete
he sets his pack on us he gifts us with graves in the air
he plays with serpents and dreams death is a master from
    Germany

your golden hair Margarete
your ashen hair Shulamith

A Visit to Belzec

I

This is Belzec,
in the East of Poland,
in the Lublin region
where the fumes of Sobibor,
Maidenek, and Treblinka still
stain the air:
smell the bodies
in the factories' smoke,
smell the sweet gas
in the clover and grass.
This is Belzec
where the death compound's gate
proclaims in Hebrew,
"Welcome to the Jewish State."
This is Belzec.
This is *SS* humor.
Curse them forever
in their black Valhalla.

II

"At 7:20 a.m. a train arrived from Lemberg with 45 wagons holding more than 6,000 people. Of these, 1,450 were already dead on arrival. Behind the small barbed-wire windows, children, young ones, frightened to death, women and men. As the train drew in, 200 Ukrainians detailed for the task tore open the doors and, laying about them with their leather whips, drove the Jews out of the cars. Instructions boomed from a loudspeaker, ordering them to remove all clothing, artificial limbs, and spectacles. . . .

"They asked what was going to happen to them. . . . Most of them knew the truth. The odor told them what their fate was to be. They walked up a small flight of steps and into the death chambers, most of them without a word, thrust forward by those behind them."

III

Listener, you have walked
into the smoke-streaked mirror
of my dream, but I can't,
or won't remember.
Did my jackboots gleam?
Did I fill out quotas?
Was it before, or after?
Did I close those doors,
or did I die?

I can still feel
iron and cold water on my fingers.
I remember running
along the bank of a river,
under trees with full summer
stars in their branches,
the sky lit up with flares
and the slight murderous arcs of tracers,
the night air wet
with the sugary odors of leaves.
Dogs barked.
Were they mine?
Were they yours?
Was I running from,
or after?

IV

"Inside the chambers SS *men were crushing the people to-
gether. 'Fill them up well,'* [Hauptsturmführer *Christian*]
*Wirth had ordered, '700 or 800 of them to every 270 square
feet.' Now the doors were closed. . . .*

*"The bodies were tossed out, blue, wet with sweat and urine,
the legs soiled with feces and menstrual blood. A couple of
dozen workers checked the mouths of the dead, which they tore
open with iron hooks. Other workers inspected anus and
genital organs in search of money, diamonds, gold, dentists
moved around hammering out gold teeth, bridges and
crowns. . . ."*

V

Listener, all words are a dream.
You have wandered into mine.
Now, as workers rummage among the corpses,
we will leave for our affairs.

This happened only once, but happened:
one Belzec morning, a boy in deathline
composed a poem, and spoke it.
The words seemed true, and saved him.
The guard's mouth fell open to wonder.

We have walked together
into the smoke-streaked
terror of Belzec,

and have walked away.
                    Now wind,
and the dawn sun,
                    lift our meeting

to where they lift the human haze

                    above that region's pines.

On an Archaic Torso of Apollo

(after Rilke)

We cannot experience that storied head
in which Apollo's eyeballs ripened like apples. Yet
his torso glows, candelabra by
whose beams his gaze, though screwed back low,

still persists, still shines. Or else his breast's
curve would never blind you, nor his loins'
slight arcs smile toward center-god, where
sperm seems candled from under.

Or else this stone would squat short, mute, dis-
figured under the shoulders' translucent fall,
nor flimmer the black light of a beast's pelt, nor

break free of its own ideas
like a star. For here there is nothing nowhere
does not see you, charge you: You must change your life.

The Uncertainty
Principle

I

Lord, must this end in prayer, or
does the Lord enter secular words?
What is in the wind? Does the wind's
red trail ever end? What is certain?
By the time Jacob Bronowski walked
into the pond—is it Your pond?
is it our pond?—what had he learned?

II

Through a whole hour of film
I'd watched Bronowski's eyes:
his glasses flashed
as though his brain were bare to sunlight.

The camera swung past tables of skulls
gathered in Göttingen by Blumenbach
over a hundred years ago:
from these bowls of old bone rose

a column of Nazi
science, calipers, iron
maggots, monographs
building ovens
to precise human
specifications.

I'd listened to Bronowski's voice
following what Rilke, speaking
of Apollo's torso called
"allen seinen Randern,"
all of its contours that broke open the atom
only to wonder, a tolerance, a
smiled estimate of error, a
limit to light to render, a
melting, a wavery withholding, what
Heisenberg won to, something like
Quine's "radical translation," language or
particle physics flying from
earth to the stars we will
worry forever.
        Still,
Erwin Schrödinger spat on his black-
shirt assistant's boots.

III

We pass beneath the connected iron arch
that still insists *Arbeit Macht Frei*
to the sky at Auschwitz,
pass to where Bronowski stands

dressed in a suit of his ideas, wearing
a black tie, stands at the edge of the pond
here in Auschwitz into which, as he says,
the ashes of millions "had been flushed,"

pass to where he stands almost
in a dream of his ideas here at the edge
of this pond in Poland, stands as though
at the ditch of his own death, says
"It was arrogance, dogma, ignorance that did this,"
and walks into the pond. The sun

candles his face, birdsong
trills from somewhere behind him.
Bronowski walks toward us, toward
the camera into the pond, bends over,
kneels, cups water in his right hand,
cups in his hand the mud, the residue of ashes,
bows here in the pond at Auschwitz.

IV

of this pond Lord
of this pond of all ponds
of silence these
words from water this
mist's gray
radiance these
first rays of the solar ovens'
undigested yellow gristle these
corridors catching the sunlight these

weeds' twist these daily
shifts these clouds this
smoke drifting waters' surfaces these
sounds escape these
voices escape I can
almost hear I
can almost hear I
cannot hear these
columns of shadows this
evening this

night now again wind
moaning past its pads'
curled edges past
its lilies' red-black
blooms its
only tongues

V

Maybe Bronowski knew that he would do this,
would walk toward the camera into the pond,
but we could not know that he would do it,
would stand in the shifting mud of the dead,
would help us to touch the watery lives of the dead,
would break the iron beat of our minds to a flutter,
a chance, would say, once and for all this
only truth that will not murder, as human
smoke rises into the blue air of Auschwitz,
would say that the atoms escape, the pond lives,
the mind's only border is this blur of tears.

The Numinous

Our language has no term that can isolate distinctly and gather into one word the total numinous impression a thing may make on the mind.

—Rudolf Otto

We are walking a sidewalk
in a German city.
We are watching gray smoke
gutter along the roofs
just as it must have
from other terrible chimneys.
We are walking our way
almost into a trance.
We are walking our way
almost into a dream
only those with blue
numbers along their wrists
can truly imagine.

Now, just in front of us, something
bursts into the air.
For a few moments
our bodies echo fear.
Pigeons, we say,
only an explosion
of beautiful blue-gray pigeons.
Only pigeons that gather

over the buildings
and begin to circle.

We are walking again, counting
all the red poinsettias
between the windowpanes
and lace curtains.
It was only
a flock of pigeons:
we can still see them
circling over the block buildings,
a hundred hearts
beating in the air.
Beautiful blue-gray pigeons.
We will always remember.

Three Fragments from Dreams

I

It was my own face shining
from the wet orange gables
of medieval Goslar.

II

In Hannover where he lay,
I visited the grave of Leibnitz.
From high above, his face
darkened in the grass
as the square clouds passed.

III

Again I walked that Freiburg corner
under the frieze
where a unicorn has stabbed the air
since Luther. The years

have worn its stone horn
down, down.
Imagine the rains.
Imagine the wars.
How many women?
It's almost impossible to remember.
Imagine the flowers in their hair.

The Tree

Not everyone can see the tree, its summer cloud of green leaves or its bare radiance under winter sunlight. Not everyone can see the tree, but it is still there, standing just outside the area that was once a name and a village: Lidice. Not everyone can see the tree, but most people, all those who can follow the forked stick, the divining rod of their heart to the tree's place, can hear it. The tree needs no wind to sound as though wind blows through its leaves. The listener hears voices of children, and of their mothers and fathers. There are moments of great joy, music, dancing, but all the sounds of the life of Lidice: drunks raving their systems, a woman moaning the old song of the toothache, strain of harness on plowhorse, whistle of flail in the golden fields. But under all these sounds is the hum of lamentation, the voices' future.

The tree is still there, but when its body fell, it was cut up and dragged away for the shredder. The tree's limbs and trunk were pulped at the papermill. And now there is a book made of this paper. When you find the book, when you turn its leaves, you will hear the villagers' voices. When you hold the leaves of this book to light, you will see the watermarks of their faces.

Poem Touching the Gestapo

Behind the apparently iron front of Teutonic organization, there was a sort of willed chaos. —*Edward Crankshaw*

The system of administration [at Auschwitz] was completely without logic. It was stupefying to see how little the orders which followed one another had in common. This was only partly due to negligence. —*Olga Lengyel*

You now, you in the next century, and the next,
hear what you'll almost remember,
see into photos where he still stands, Himmler,
whose round and puffy face concealed visions,

cortege of the condemned winding toward Birkenau,

and how to preserve Jews' heads in hermetically sealed tins,

der Ritter, knight, *treuer Heinrich*,

visions of death's head returning in Reich's light,
the Aryan skull ascending the misformed skull of the beast,
the Jew, Gypsy, lunatic, Slav, syphilitic, homosexual,

100

ravens and wolves, the Blood Flag, composer Wagner
whose heart went out to frogs, who, like Martin Luther,
wanted to drive Jews "like mad dogs out of the land,"

Heydrich dead but given Lidice,
Mengele injecting dye into Jewish eyes—
Ist das die deutsche Kultur?—
this vomit at last this last
cleansing and an end to it,
if it is possible, if I will it now,

Lebensborn stud farms, *Rassenschande*, *Protocols
of the Elders of Zion*, *SS* dancing in nuns' clothes,

Otto Ohlendorf, who left his Berlin desk to command
Einsatsgruppe D and roam the East killing
one million undesirables in less than two years' time,

lamenting the mental strain on his men,
the stench of inadequate graves,
corpses that fouled themselves in the gas vans,

the graves rupturing, backs, backs of heads, limbs
above ground as they are here, if I will it now,

the day-in, day-out shootings of Jews, some attractive,
brave, even intelligent, but to be dealt with
in strict military order, not like at Treblinka where
gas chambers were too small, and converted gas vans' engines
sometimes wouldn't start, the thousands already
packed into the showers for history,

their hands up so more would fit, and smaller children
thrown in at the space left at the top,
and we knew they were all dead, said Hoess of Auschwitz,
when the screaming stopped,

Endlosung, Edelweiss, Lebensraum, Mussulmen, Cyklon B,

"and his large blue eyes like stars," as Goebbels wrote,
and the Fuehrer's films of conspirators on meathooks,

we cannot keep it all, an end to it,
visions of loyal Heinrich, what engineer Grabe saw at Dubno,
he and two postmen allowed to watch, the vans arriving,
a father holding his boy and pointing to that sky,
explaining something, when the *SS* shouted and counted off
twenty more or less and pushed them behind the earth mound,

Stahlhelm, Horst Wessel, Goering in a toga at *Karinhalle,*
redbeard Barbarossa rising,

that father and son, and the sister remembered by Grabe
as pointing to herself, slim girl with black hair,
and saying, "twenty-three years old,"
as Grabe behind the mound saw a tremendous grave,

the holy orders of the *SS,* Lorelei, the Reichstag fire,
Befehl ist Befehl, Anne Frank in Belsen, jackboots, Krupp,

bodies wedged together tightly on top of one another,
some still moving, lifting arms to show life,

102

the pit two-thirds full, maybe a thousand dead,
the German who did the shooting sitting at the edge,
his gun on his knees, and he's smoking a cigarette,
as more naked victims descend steps cut in the pit's clay,
clamber over the heads of those already dead there,
and lay themselves down. Grabe heard some speak
in low voice, . . . listen . . .
before the shooting, the twitching, the spurting blood,

competition for the highest extermination counts,
flesh sometimes splashed on field reports,
seldom time even to save skulls with perfect teeth
for perfect paperweights,

his will be done, and kill them, something deeper dying,
but kill them, cognac and nightmares but kill them,
Eichmann's "units," the visions, the trenches
angled with ditches to drain off the human fat,

the twins and dwarfs, the dissidents *aus Nacht und Nebel,*

Professor Dr. Hans Kramer of the University of Munster
who stood on a platform to channel new arrivals—
gas chamber, forced labor, gas chamber—and later,
in special action, saw live women and children thrown into pits
and soaked with gasoline and set on fire—
Kramer, a doctor, who kept a diary filled with
"excellent lunch: tomato soup, half a hen with
potatoes and red cabbage, sweets and marvellous vanilla ice,"
while trains kept coming, families with
photograph albums falling out of the cars, the books

of the camps and prisons, the albums imprinting the air,
as here, we close our eyes, and the rain falling from photos
onto the earth, dried in the sun and raining again,
no way to them now but this way, willed chaos,

visions deeper in time than even the graves of the murdered
daughter who tells us her age,
in the round face of the man with glasses and weak chin,
Himmler, *Geheime Staats Polizie*, twisting his snake ring,

as now the millions approach, these trucks arriving with more,
these trains arriving with more, from *Prinz Albrecht Strasse*,
from the mental strain on Ohlendorf's men,
from the ravine at Babi Yar, from the future,
from the pond at Auschwitz and the clouds of ash,
from numberless mass graves where Xian prayer and Kaddish
now slow into undersong, O Deutschland, my soul, this soil
resettled forever here, remembered, poem touching the Gestapo,
the families, the children, the visions,
the visions . . .

My Holocaust Songs

I

Some split *SS* backbones with axes,
but who can praise them?
Some filed like sheep into the corridors of the swastika,
but who can blame them?
Some found smoke's way to the cosmos,
but who can see them?
Some rose earth's way to grass and pond-pads,
but who can know them?

II

Dead Jew goldpiece in German eye,
dead Jew shovel in German shed,
dead Jew book in German hand,
dead Jew hat on German head,
dead Jew violin in German ear,
dead Jew linen on German skin,
dead Jew blood in German vein,
dead Jew breath in German lung,
dead Jew love in German brain.

III

Break down again, songs, break down
into pure melody, wind's way,
history sung in leaves almost lost,
atoms of singing darkness, the meanings,
the wailing songs of the holocaust,
themselves dying, returning with spring, the bleeding
notes, break down, break down again, my songs.

Simple Truths

When a man has grown a body,
a body to carry with him
through nature for as long as he can,
when this body is taken from him
by other men and women who happen to be,
this time, in uniform,
then it is clear he has experienced
an act of barbarism,

and when a man has a wife,
a wife to love for as long as he lives,
when this wife is marked with a yellow star
and driven into a chamber she will never leave alive,
then this is murder,
so much is clear,

and when a woman has hair,
when her hair is shorn and her scalp bleeds,
when a woman has children,
children to love for as long as she lives,
when the children are taken from her,
when a man and his wife and their children

are put to death in a chamber of gas,
or with pistols at close range, or are starved,
or beaten, or injected by the thousands,
or ripped apart, by the thousands, by the millions,

it is clear that where we are
is Europe, in our century, during the years
from nineteen-hundred and thirty-five
to nineteen-hundred and forty-five
after the death of Jesus, who spoke of a different order,
but whose father, who is our father,
if he is our father,
if we must speak of him as father,
watched, and witnessed, and knew,

and when we remember,
when we touch the skin of our own bodies,
when we open our eyes into dream
or within the morning shine of sunlight
and remember what was taken
from these men, from these women,
from these children gassed and starved
and beaten and thrown against walls
and made to walk the valley
of knives and icepicks and otherwise
exterminated in ways appearing to us almost
beyond even the maniacal human imagination,
then it is clear that this is the German Reich,
during approximately ten years of our lord's time,

and when we read a book of these things,
when we hear the names of the camps,

108

when we see the films of the bulldozed dead
or the film of one boy struck on the head
with a club in the hands
of a German doctor who will wait
some days for the boy's skull to knit, and will enter
the time in his ledger, and then
take up the club to strike the boy again,
and wait some weeks for the boy's skull to knit,
and enter the time in his ledger again,
and strike the boy again,
and so on, until the boy, who,
at the end of the film of his life
can hardly stagger forward toward the doctor,
does die, and the doctor
enters exactly the time of the boy's death in his ledger,

when we read these things or see them,
then it is clear to us that this
happened, and within the lord's allowance, this
work of his minions, his poor
vicious dumb German victims twisted
into the swastika shapes of trees struck by lightning,
on this his earth, if he is our father,
if we must speak of him in this way,
this presence above us, within us, this
mover, this first cause, this spirit, this
curse, this bloodstream and brain-current, this
unfathomable oceanic ignorance of ourselves, this
automatic electric Aryan swerve, this

fortune that you and I were not the victims, this
luck that you and I were not the murderers, this

sense that you and I are clean and understand, this
stupidity that gives him breath, gives him life
as we kill them all, as we killed them all.

New Year's Eve: The Bridge

If the new year can come,
it must come here,
under the ribcage,
under the ice below,
under the black water,
if it can come.

One night in the North Atlantic,
hearing the ocean's call
for depth, space, I leaned
over the ship's lowest rail—
the moon drifted, blurred
tattoo. I pictured, Lord,

You, Your vast
indefinite face, heard
Your heartbeat in the swells:
tell me, I prayed,
and almost entered,
but learned, or lost courage,

or awakened. Lord,
Your desertion, Your clouded grace,
Your death camps still
hover over the seas, over
this slash of the new world's water,
and will. That year I prayed

that I was weak, a fallen human,
fool, not Your minion, not released
from nothingness for Your
amusement, blessed
to kill. As millions of stars
rise in the black heavens

(motes in Your myriad eye),
I pray this still,
and pray for earthly wisdom,
that the new year can come.

Ewige Melodien

Something: dead friends' welcoming whispers? but
    something: wooden windbells, chimes? but
something: my skin soft now Lord we are all dead but

something: music lower than birdsong but
    something: our throats that screamed are soft now and
something: thrum of dew drying from grassblades? but

something: our fingers that clawed are soft now and
    something: rustle-of-grain sound somehow yellow? but
something: our lungs that burst with blood are soft now and

something: trees filling with windsong? but
    something: deep cello timbre, low resinous hum? but
something: jaw muscles soft now, neck muscles, tongues but

something: brain hymn, bodiless heartbeat? but
    something: we should have known this
something: . . . the melodies begin . . .

The Vapor

Events wound down to chaos.
Wanting to leave some trace,
Dietrich Bonhoeffer wrote his name
in his copy of Plutarch.
That book finds its way home,
his own life glowing from the Nazi dark.

When we touch the book of such a man,
when we hear his hymn
"O faithful God prepare my grave,"
or his last spoken words, "This is the end,
but now I begin to live,"
we breathe the Erika vapor of those dead

who may come to comfort, and to bless
when next the runic lightning *SS*
slashes down. He tells us God is helpless
here in the world unless we share
His suffering, and thereby raise
all grief to holiness, to praise.

The murdered German pastor
who would have killed the Fuehrer
still sends us letters from his cell.
Sometimes, all God's prison bulbs go black.
Dietrich mists and wipes his glasses, sits back,
remembers a word that lights another candle.

114

The Halo

A sister tells the story of Chicha at Auschwitz,
how Irma Grese, that *SS* aberration of beauty,
forced Chicha to hold two rocks high,
rocks she would die for if they fell. . . .

Where did the girl in bone-stretched skin find strength?
Her arms trembled together at elbows to hold steady.
God, keep her arms straight, our souls riveted to hers,
for this is the hour of good against evil. . . .

The camp dies into grayish dusk and blacker shadow.
We see a halo glowing around her shriveled body.
From then to now, Chicha pushes the rocks upward until
the torturer returns, says, "Put those rocks down."

The Children

I do not think we can save them.
I remember, within my dream, repeating
I do not think we can save them.
But our cars follow one another
over the cobblestones. Our dim
headlamps, yellow in fog, brush past,
at the center of a market square,
its cathedral's great arched doors.
I know, now, this is a city
in Germany, two years
after the Crystal Night. I think ahead
to the hospital, the children.
I do not think we can save them.

Inside this dream,
in a crystal dashboard vase,
one long-stemmed rose unfolds
strata of soft red light.
Its petals fall, tears, small
flames. I cup my palm to hold them,
and my palm fills to its brim,
will overflow.

Is this the secret, then? . . .
Now I must spill the petal light, and drive.

We are here, in front of the hospital,
our engines murmuring. Inside,
I carry a child under each arm,
down stairs, out to my car.
One's right eyeball hangs on its cheek
on threads of nerve and tendon,
but he still smiles, and I love him.
The other has lost her chin—
I can see straight down her throat
to where her heart beats
black-red, black-red.
I do not think we can save them.

I am the last driver in this procession.
Many children huddle in my car.
We have left the city. Our lights
tunnel the fog beneath arches of linden,
toward Bremerhaven, toward
the western shore.
I do not think we can save them.
This time, at the thought, lights
whirl in my mirror, intense
fear, and the screams of sirens.
I begin to cry, for myself, for the children.
A voice in my dream says
this was the midnight you were born. . . .

Later, something brutal happened, of course,
but as to this life I had to, I woke,

and cannot, or will not, remember.
But the children, of course, were murdered,
their graves lost, their names lost,
even those two faces lost to me. Still,
this morning, inside the engine of my body,
for once, as I wept and breathed deep,
relief, waves of relief, as though the dreamed

rose would spill its petals forever.
I prayed thanks. For one night, at least,
I tried to save the children,
to keep them safe in my own body,
and knew I would again.   Amen.

The Swastika Poems

They appeared, overnight,
on our steps, like frost stars
on our windows, their strict
crooked arms pointing

this way and that, scare-
crows, skeletons, limbs
akimbo. My father
cursed in his other tongue

and scraped them off,
or painted them over.
My mother bit her lips.
This was all a wonder,

and is: how that sign
came to be a star flashing
above our house when I dreamed,
how the star's bone-white light

first ordered me to follow,
how the light began

like the oak's leaves in autumn
to yellow, how the star now

sometimes softens the whole sky
with its twelve sides,
how the pen moves with it,

how the heart beats with it,
how the eyes remember.

This Night

Which is our star this night?
Belsen is bathed in blue,
every footworn lane, every
strand of wire, pale blue.
The guards' bodies,
the prisoners' bodies—all
black and invisible. Only
their pale blue eyes
float above the lanes
or between the wires.
Or they are all dead,
and these are the blue eyes of those
haunted by what happened here.
Which eyes are yours,
which mine? Even
blue-eyed crows
drift the darkness overhead. Even
blue-eyed worms
sip dew from the weeping leaves
of the black Erika
over the graves. . . .
But now, at once, every

eye, every blue light
closes. As we do.
For rest. For now.
Which was our star this night?

NOTES

The quotation from Susan Sontag used as epigraph for this book is from her discussion of Rolfe Hochhuth's play *The Deputy* in *Against Interpretation* (New York, 1966).

"A Snapshot of My Father, 1928": "Dutchman" was a term used by Americans to label all those immigrants, including Germans, who sounded as though they spoke Dutch. The word often carried more than a little derision with it.

"Letter to Hansjörg Greiner": "Stalingrader" was the general term for anyone who took part in that battle. Greiner, before volunteering for or being ordered to the Russian front, worked at the Propaganda Ministry in Berlin. After finishing this poem, I found him listed as one of about fifty participants at Goebbels' almost daily conferences from 1939–1941 (*The Secret Conferences of Dr. Goebbels,* ed. Willi A. Boelcke, New York, 1970).

"Men in History": Much of this poem is based on Albert Speer's memoir *Inside the Third Reich* (New York, 1970).

"Three Relations": Saul K. Padover was an American intelligence officer in psychological warfare who moved into Germany immediately behind our armies. Parts I and III of this poem follow stories related to him and reported in his *Experiment in Germany* (New York, 1946). The former is spoken by a German woman who had seen Hitler at Aachen, and the latter by a Frenchman who was forced to work at Sachsenhausen in 1944. Part II of my poem is based on passages in *The Beasts of the Earth,* by Georg M. Karst (pseud.), trans. by Emil Lengyel (New York, 1942).

"A New Bible": The epigraph from Primo Levi is from his *If This Is Man* (New York, 1959). . . . . It was at Treblinka where a clock whose hands pointed to three was painted on a false wall at the arrival "station."

"Passover: The Injections": I wrote this poem after reading Susan Fromberg Schaeffer's powerful and moving novel *Anya* (New York, 1974).

"The Car": Hitler's fantasy is mentioned in *Treblinka*, by Jean-Francois Steiner (New York, 1967).

"The Hair: Jacob Korman's Story": This poem is based on an experience related by one of the survivors in the study by Dorothy Rabinowitz, *New Lives: Survivors of the Holocaust Living in America* (New York, 1976).

"The Funnel: Speech to Jews at Treblinka by Kurt Franz": Commandant Franz' speech is also reported in Steiner's *Treblinka*. The speech is insane, surely, and my parodical form is insane, obscene. I realize that this is a dimension of several poems in *Erika*, presentation itself as obscenity, as in the four-syllable lines of the earlier "The Car," and in the shapes of the later "The Fountain" and "Blue."

"Dark in the Reich of the Blond": I wrote this poem after reading *The Third Reich of Dreams*, by Charlotte Beradt (Chicago, 1968).

"Kotov": I've been unable to locate the book in which I found the history of Ivan Ivanovitch Kotov, but his story is a true one.

"A History of Germany under National Socialism": The rubble of this poem is the rubble of Goering's Prussian estate. *The Reich Marshall*, by Leonard Mosley (Garden City, 1974), though too sympathetic to Goering, captures the cloying Aryan melodrama of the Carin-Hermann relationship, from their first meeting in a Swedish castle to when her skull is kicked up in the ruins of the mausoleum he had built for her.

"The Census": Leo Haas's painting may be found in *The Artists of Terezin*, by Gerald Green (New York, 1978). . . . A poem such as "The Census," easily misunderstood, almost unstable, discursive as it is, having a great deal on its mind at once, is primarily about the consciousness it embodies, one in the present act of discovering what it knows, and how, finally, it can stop talking, despite its obsessions, for at least a while. "Simple Truths," another such poem, begins as rationally as possible, but then, it seems to me, becomes hysterical.

"A Voice from the Night at Belsen": Fania Fenelon in *Playing for Time* (New York, 1977) mentions the girl who cried out for her jewels.

"Darkness": Lev Bezymenski's *The Death of Adolf Hitler* (London, 1968) describes the autopsies performed on charred bodies dug up by the Russians from the Chancellery garden. In *Adolf Hitler* (New York, 1973), Colin Cross argues that the Russian findings, particularly in regard to the body supposed to be Hitler's, are disputable. . . . When I first published this poem as a chapbook in 1976, I wrote a note to accompany it, an apology. I would like to quote the two paragraphs of this note here:

I remember that "Darkness" was an evening's outpouring. For seven or eight years I'd been reading about WWII and the Holocaust with a constant sense of disbelief, shaking my head as I read, thinking that all of this could not have happened. All of my reading experiences, all of those walks through German cities and woods during 1971-2 when I spent a year there where it all began, a day at Belsen I'll never forget—I am there now as I write, the Erika over the mass graves beginning to pulse with spring—all these things led to the voice of fragment and obsession that is "Darkness." That same evening, just before the poem, in effect, wrote itself, I had seen the film The Man in the Glass Booth, *its strange psychological leaps, and had walked home in a moonless darkness, my mind whirling.*

I am worried about the poem. What does it do? Where does it go? The speaker (the self I was, the selves, as I wrote) begins with the fear that he will lose the camps, forget them. But his words turn to say that it is not just that he is afraid he will not be able to hold the victims in his memory: it seems to me that he is afraid that he will miss the drama and excitement of that whole history. From this point on, there is no mental censorship of what happens as the speaker talks, as he projects his body into the bunker, as he imagines a grotesque and even perverse exhumation of his Fuehrer. (I hear, now, in some lines, my remembrance of the Russian autopsy report on that body dug up in the Chancellery garden.) The poem is haunted with cattlecars and skin lampshades. Within a book, finished, that will be called The Swastika Poems, *it says, if anything, something much of the book tries to articulate. It says now, says that this is all with us now, all these impulses, this sensibility, moral and murderous and sexual at the same time. I believe that such recognitions are necessary, however distasteful they are. I am worried about "Darkness." But, in its own way, it says now, says that this is still with us. As it is.*

"Erika": The epigraph from Peter Weiss is from "My Place," an

125

essay about a day he spent at Auschwitz, in *German Writing Today,* ed. Christopher Middleton (Baltimore, 1967).

"Blue": The quotation from Elie Wiesel is from *Night* (New York, 1960).

"Mandorla": A mandorla is an oval medieval painting, probably one from which, in this case, the likeness of Jesus has faded or been cut. Paul Celan, or the "ich" of the poem, begins "In der Mandel," associating the German word for almond with his title. The more I hear this poem, the more haunting it becomes. The eighth line, for example, suggests the eternity of the Jewish people, their death in the camps, and their inability to become wise. The penultimate line may expand this into a kind of holocaust of ignorance for all humanity. The last line is filled with horror and beauty. . . . I'm indebted to "Manifestations of the Holocaust: Interpreting Paul Celan" by Jerry Glenn in *Books Abroad,* 46, 1 (Winter 1972), 25-30.

"Death Fugue": I'm familiar with translations of Celan's poem by Michael Hamburger, Christopher Middleton, and Joachim Neugroschel. While many of my words must of necessity be theirs, I've brought into my translation emphases and rhythms different from theirs that I feel in the original German.

"A Visit to Belzec": Sections II and IV are taken from Richard Grunberger's *Hitler's SS* (New York, 1972). . . . It may be that because we as human beings, in ineffable and mysterious ways, share responsibility for the evils of history, a stance of moral superiority in poetry is often insufferable and always wrong. I know, at the same time, that poems in *Erika* slant in in different ways to condemn. Perhaps the most *direct* damning takes place in two lines in this poem: "Curse them forever / in their black Valhalla." . . . In *The Trains* (Worcester, Ma.: Metacom Press, 1981), I published the April 29, 1972 entry of a journal I kept in Germany that year. For the questions it raises, I repeat that entry here:

Worked at a poem last night. Don't know if it will come to anything. Haven't written a line since December, and I've learned: It can go away. It's easy to forget the concentration and awareness I used to snap into. I used to know what previous words and lines were doing and saying as I moved to the next line. But my brain is already going at different frequencies, and after just several months. Hard to explain. Since Belsen. Also, maybe that place knocked a lot of the fancy out of me, the relativistic dance. A moral poetry is so much out

126

of favor that even the unconscious of American poets rebels against saying that men can be more than animals, that civilization means the recognition and control of certain instincts, that there is a divine moral order, that it is the psychotic who looks forward to destruction and genocide to complement his own psychosis, that man is an ongoing experiment in whom God is interested, that we must not give up to weariness and Weltschmerz and nihilism, that "moral" works of art can actually help to build a consensus for moral action. This kind of simplicity, too, will be twisted by the fashionable. Lord, help me to rid myself of the desire to kill other people, for my spirit wants to declare that desire alien.

I do not know how—are there other than slippery and ambiguous modern models?—to write that kind of poem, or am afraid to write it. But I have the feeling that most of the American "poets" of my generation are just fooling around, that we are indulging ourselves, throwing off thin and misty and evasive things, giving up to a vapid surrealism, telling ourselves that our foolish poems are really serious, dancing around the edges of amorality, declaring that we cannot communicate with one another, that all is lost, that this is the age of situational ethics and play. I have a feeling that one smell of the human smoke at Auschwitz would cure this.

Maybe the poem that should be written would actually say that Auschwitz was wrong under the heavens, and wrong within laws of organic nature on earth, and wrong under indwelling human laws. A prayer: Lord, give me the will and strength to be what a man is meant to be. All sorts of assumptions behind that prayer. Lord, let me be willing to assume the assumptions behind that prayer, and, Lord, let them be the truth of your Being.

"The Uncertainty Principle": Willard Van Orman Quine is the author of *Word and Object* (Cambridge, Ma., 1960), a study of the possibilities of precise communications through language. The quoted phrase suggests to me that our individual meanings for words are various and even eccentric enough to require constant and strenuous translation as we try to reach one another.

"The Numinous": The epigraph is from Otto's *The Idea of the Holy*, translated by John W. Harvey (New York, 1958).

"The Tree": Lidice was a Czechoslovakian village entirely destroyed by the Nazis in 1942 in reprisal for the assassination of the area's Gestapo "Protector" Reinhardt Heydrich by Czech patriots.

All males of fifteen or older were shot; women were sent to concentration camps; physically acceptable children were Germanized while the others were also sent to camps. The village, in effect, disappeared.

"Poem Touching the Gestapo": The epigraphs are from Edward Crankshaw's *Gestapo* (New York, 1956), and Olga Lengyel's *Five Chimneys* (St. Albans, Hertfordshire, 1972). Although most readers will not be familiar with all the tags and catchwords associated with various abominations of the Third Reich that pour out of the poem's voice, any good history of the period will explain these things, and definitions would prove awkward, perhaps even unnecessary, here.

"The Halo": The story of Chicha is based on passages in *Fragments of Isabella: A Memoir of Auschwitz*, by Isabella Leitner (New York, 1978).

WILLIAM HEYEN

William Heyen was born November 1, 1940, in Brooklyn, New York, and raised on Long Island. He received his Ph.D. from Ohio University in 1967, when he returned to teach at the State University of New York College at Brockport, his undergraduate alma mater, where he is now Professor of English. He edited *A Profile of Theodore Roethke* (1971), and *American Poets in 1976* (1976). He spent 1971-2 in Germany as a Senior Fulbright Lecturer in American Literature. His recent honors include the annual *Ontario Review* Poetry Prize (1977), the Eunice Tietjens Memorial Prize from *Poetry* magazine (1978), a John Simon Guggenheim Memorial Fellowship in poetry (1977-78), and the Witter Bynner Prize for Poetry from the American Academy and Institute of Arts and Letters (1982).